Totally WACKY FACTS ABOUT ANCIENT HISTORY

CARI MEISTER

ALEXANDER THE GREAT NAMED 70 CITIES AFTER HIMSELF.

Well, **I AM** Alexander **THE GREAT** after all!

He named one city after his horse, **BUCEPHELA.**

He owned 5,500,000 square kilometres (2,123,562 square miles) of the ancient world.

THAT'S MORE LAND THAN ANY OTHER RULER IN HISTORY HAS OWNED.

Alexander was so rich it took **20,000 MULES** and **5,000 CAMELS** to move his jewels and gold.

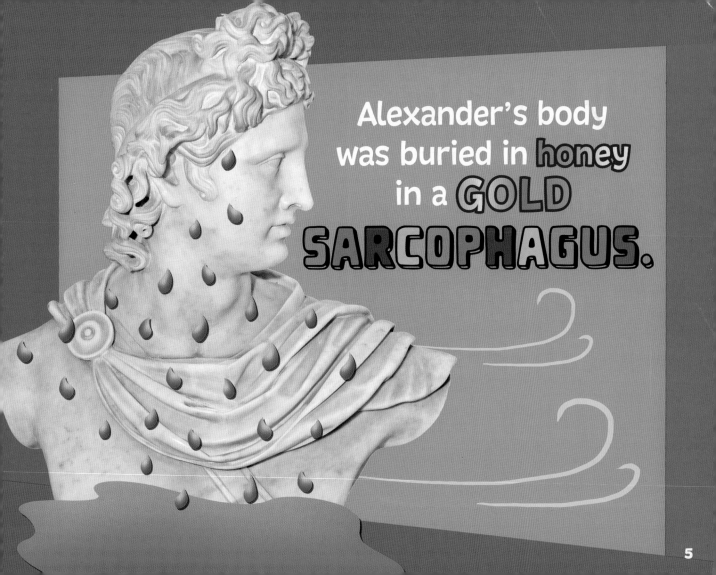

Alexander's body was buried in **honey** in a **GOLD SARCOPHAGUS.**

IN ANCIENT
ROME ONLY
EMPERORS
WERE ALLOWED
TO WEAR
PURPLE
TOGAS.

It took 10,000 MUREX MOLLUSCS to make the dye for one purple toga.

The first EMPEROR OF CHINA was buried with an estimated 8,000 TERRACOTTA SOLDIERS.

FARMERS DISCOVERED THE TOMB WHILE DIGGING A WELL IN 1974 – BUT THE ACTUAL TOMB HAS NEVER BEEN OPENED.

Archaeologists believe the tomb has a river of mercury running through it!

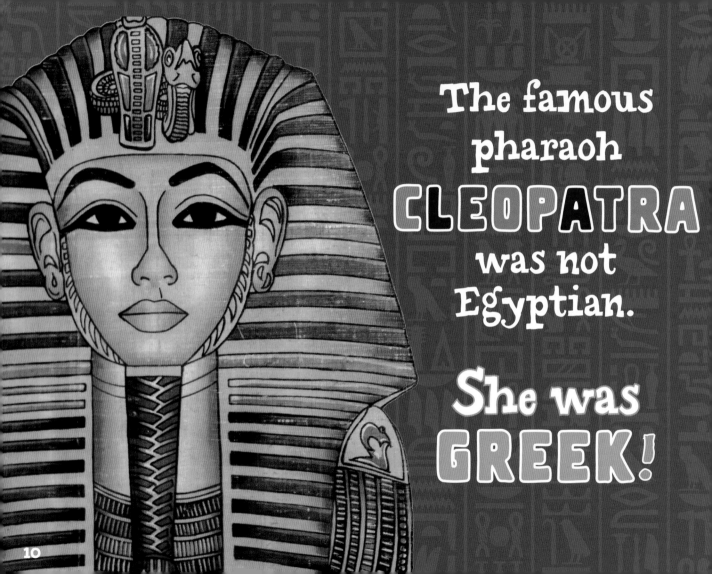

The famous pharaoh **CLEOPATRA** was not Egyptian.

She was **GREEK!**

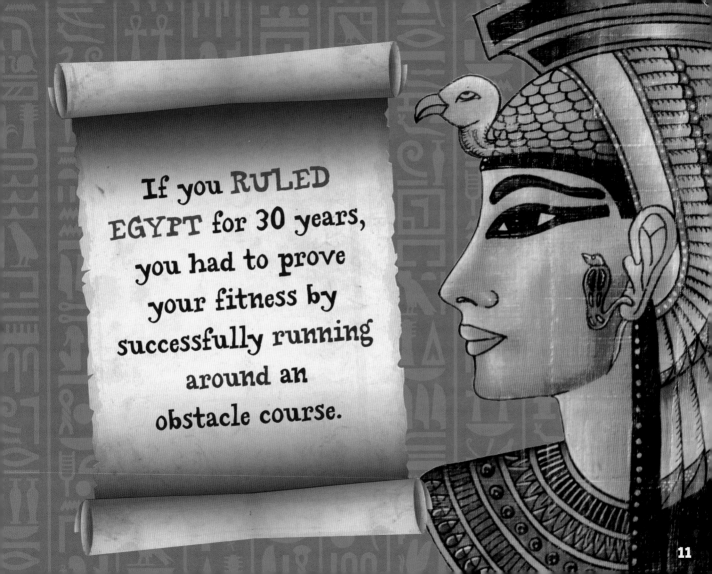

If you RULED EGYPT for 30 years, you had to prove your fitness by successfully running around an obstacle course.

The famous pharaoh Hatshepsut married her half brother to become queen.

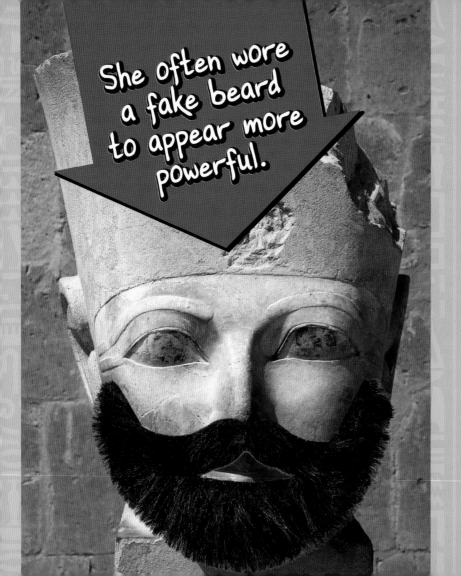

She often wore a fake beard to appear more powerful.

She is shown as TRIM and ATHLETIC on her sarcophagus.

But historians believe she was BIG and BALDING.

13

ANCIENT EGYPTIANS MUMMIFIED CATS TO PLEASE THEIR GODS.

SCIENTISTS FOUND ONE TOMB THAT HELD 80,000 CAT MUMMIES!

EGYPTIANS ALSO MUMMIFIED MICE so the cats would have something to chase in the afterlife.

THE GREAT ROMAN ORATOR LUCIUS LICINIUS CRASSUS BURIED HIS PET EEL WITH A NECKLACE AND EARRINGS.

Favourite pet
of the ancient Chinese:
THE CRICKET.

EGYPTIANS

had all kinds of pets including hawks, ibises, lions and baboons.

Are you an
ANCIENT GREEK
with no money?

Can't afford a real
ANIMAL SACRIFICE?

DON'T WORRY!
You can sacrifice an animal
made of dough instead!

SUMERIANS

thought the **spirit of a dead person** could enter a **living person** through his or her ear.

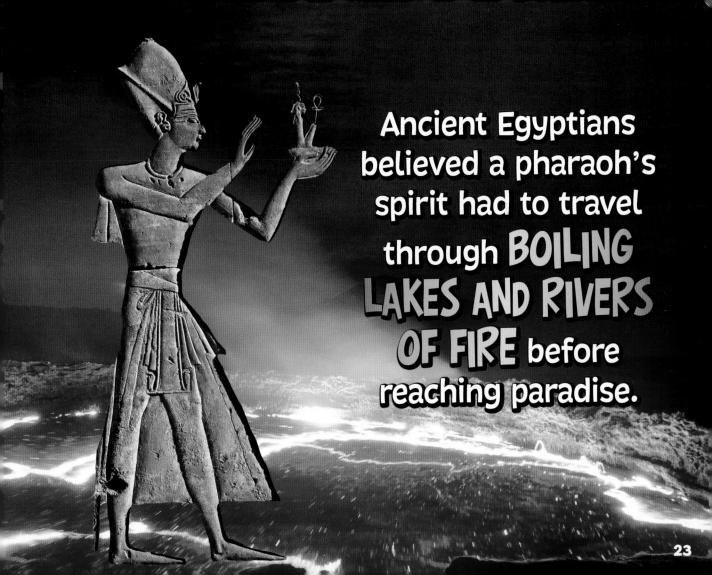

Ancient Egyptians believed a pharaoh's spirit had to travel through BOILING LAKES AND RIVERS OF FIRE before reaching paradise.

No one is quite sure where the BIBLE'S GARDEN OF EDEN was located.

According to the Bible, the deck on Noah's ark was the size of 36 tennis courts!

The Bible says a chest called the Ark of the Covenant holds the tablets of the **TEN COMMANDMENTS.** People still search for it today.

GREEK BABIES WERE WRAPPED IN TIGHT CLOTH SO THEIR BONES WOULD GROW STRAIGHT.

In some ancient cultures, babies were fed WINE AND HONEY.

WHY would they feed us that stuff?

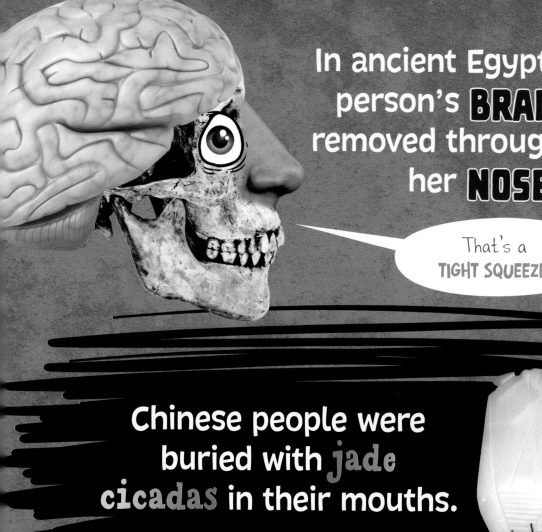

In ancient Egypt a dead person's **BRAIN** was removed through his or her **NOSE.**

That's a **TIGHT SQUEEZE!**

Chinese people were buried with jade cicadas in their mouths.

MOST EGYPTIAN PHARAOHS WERE BURIED WITH BLACK STONES FOR EYES.

RAMSES IV

was buried with onions for his eyes.

Didn't they know onions make me CRY?

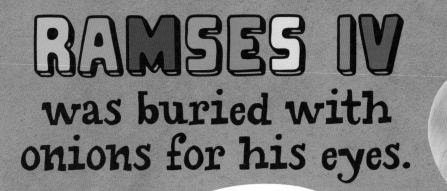

In ancient China body armour was made from

STRONG PAPER.

EARLY ROMAN MILITARY SANDALS HAD NAILHEADS FOR CLEATS.

SPARTAN ARMOUR WAS **BRONZE** AND WEIGHED 14 TO 23 KILOGRAMS (40 TO 50 POUNDS)!

SCYTHIAN WARRIORS USED BARBED ARROWHEADS AGAINST THEIR ENEMIES.

They also tipped their arrows in snake venom and animal dung.

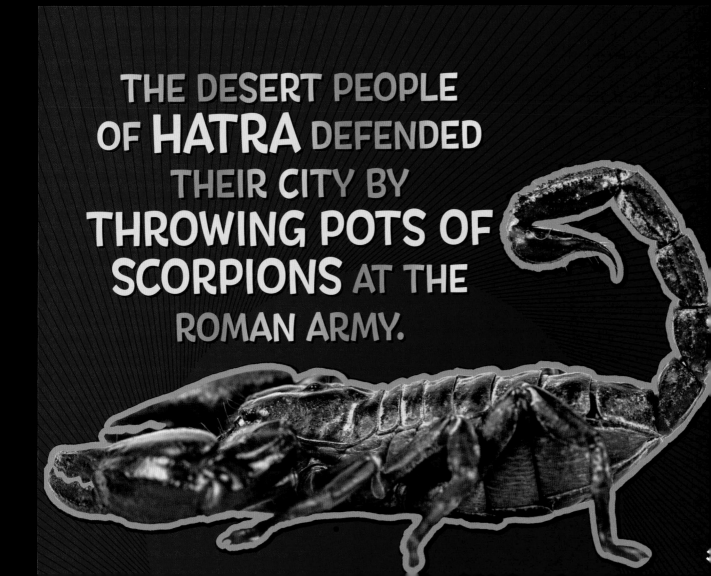

KEEP SHOOTING! I'll take all your arrows, please.

The ANCIENT CHINESE used mannequins in battle to collect their enemies' arrows.

Early **Chinese** **spies** flew on large kites to gather information about their enemies.

The only honourable job for Spartan males? Soldier.

Weak Spartan babies were left outside to die.

What if **I WANT TO BE** a gardener?

SPARTAN BOYS WERE TAKEN FROM THEIR FAMILIES AT AGE 7 TO BEGIN MILITARY TRAINING.

39

Ancient Greeks were scared of

ZOMBIES.

BEWARE OF ZOMBIES!

ANCIENT ROMANS applied cobwebs, honey and vinegar to wounds to help them heal.

Some
ANCIENT NATIVE AMERICANS
used animal tendons
to suture cuts.

KNOW SOMEONE WHO WETS THE BED?

Try the ancient cure of placing a bag of mouse bones around the person's neck!

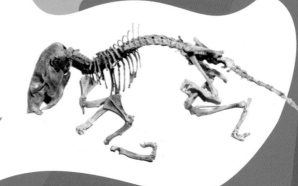

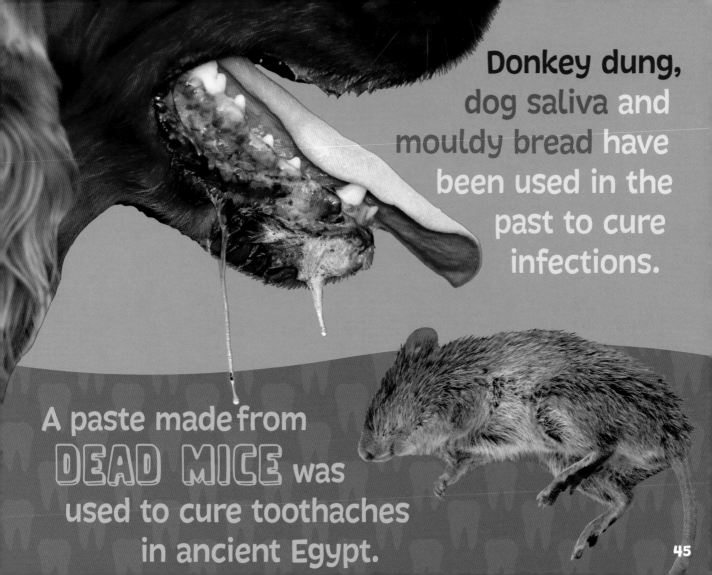

Donkey dung, dog saliva and mouldy bread have been used in the past to cure infections.

A paste made from DEAD MICE was used to cure toothaches in ancient Egypt.

45

Roman gladiators rarely ate meat – they were mostly vegetarian!

Gladiators enjoyed a sports drink made from vinegar and burned plants.

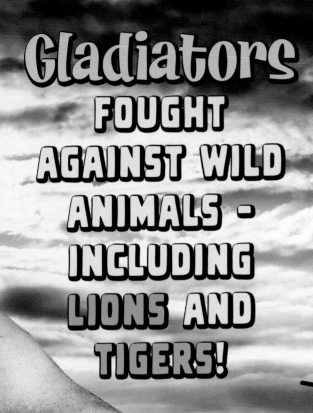

Gladiators
FOUGHT AGAINST WILD ANIMALS - INCLUDING LIONS AND TIGERS!

KIDS PLAYED WITH **CLAY FIGURINES** MADE TO LOOK LIKE FAMOUS GLADIATORS.

When an ancient Egyptian died, people often left GAMES in the tomb for the afterlife.

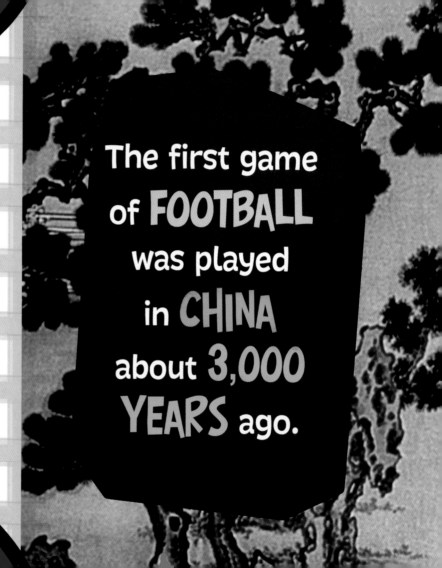

People recently found a 5,000-year-old CARVED STONE PUZZLE BALL in SCOTLAND. It was similar to the modern Rubik's Cube.

The first game of FOOTBALL was played in CHINA about 3,000 YEARS ago.

Ancient Romans were the first to record seeing UFOS.

The **ANCIENT CHINESE** invented a seismograph to detect **EARTHQUAKES** before they happened.

Chinese seismograph

56

THE FIRST NONELECTRIC **BATTERIES** WERE INVENTED MORE THAN 2,000 YEARS AGO.

Another ancient invention:

BOOMERANGS have been around for over 20,000 years!

ATILLA THE HUN WAS A FEARLESS, MURDEROUS WARRIOR WHO RAVAGED LANDS DURING THE 5TH CENTURY.

His gaze was SO TERRIFYING that people would run away in horror.

On his wedding night, he choked to death from a nosebleed.

Roman toilets

ROMANS LIKED TO POO IN GROUPS.

In **ANCIENT ROME** **urine** was used to clean clothes.

61

If an **EGYPTIAN PEASANT** was deemed too lazy, officials would cut off his toe or finger.

Once a year ROMANS had a big party where slaves and owners would switch places.

UNUSUAL JOBS in the Ancient World:

Do I look LIKE I NEED TO BE KEPT?

public pig keeper

armpit-hair plucker

perfume seller

nomenclator – a poorly paid worker who remembered stuff for others

praegustator – a taster; he tasted food before royalty ate it, to make sure it wasn't poisoned

65

ANCIENT GREEKS used crushed mulberries to make their **cheeks rosier.**

They also wore **FAKE EYEBROWS** made of musk-ox fur.

Teeth that had been painted black were considered beautiful in ANCIENT CHINA.

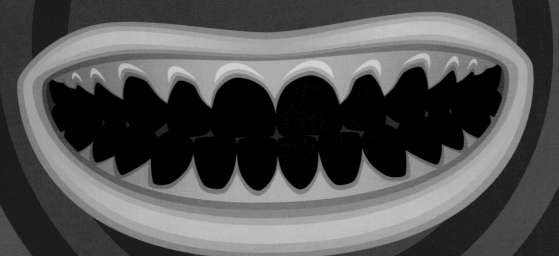

Women in **ANCIENT CHINA** polished their nails with **RAW EGG.**

ANCIENT EGYPTIANS LOVED WEARING WIGS.

Ancient Romans dyed their hair **BLACK** using rotten leeches and **SQUID INK**.

Ancient Romans applied a mix of **ASHES** and **PIGEON POO** to make their hair look **BLONDE.**

EGYPTIAN WOMEN got TATTOOS to protect their unborn babies.

Early tattoo "ink" was made from soot, rust and coloured sand.

TAHITIANS OFTEN COVERED THEIR WHOLE BODIES IN TATTOOS.

During a **SYRIAN KING'S WEDDING**, people adorned goats with silver necklaces and let them roam around the city.

I wish the **KING WOULD GET MARRIED** more often!

The earliest **WEDDING RINGS** were made from **BRAIDED GRASS.**

In **ANCIENT ROME,** a wedding was not official until the couple **KISSED.** (EWWW!)

ROMANS dined while lying on couches.

THINGS ANCIENT PEOPLE DRANK:

WINE sweetened with lead (Many people were poisoned accidentally.)

MILK from yaks, donkeys, zebras, horses **and** sheep

THE OLDEST SKIS
(over 6,000 years old)
were found in **RUSSIA.**

Early **ICE SKATES** were made by strapping **ANIMAL BONES** to your **FEET.**

DARIUS THE GREAT, KING OF PERSIA,

built a magnificent palace in the middle of the desert. It even had a **SEWAGE SYSTEM!**

The entrance had a **WIDE STAIRCASE** that horses could walk up so royalty didn't have to touch the dusty ground.

In **TURKEY** there is an ancient 18-storey **UNDERGROUND CITY**.

Some **JAPANESE SCIENTISTS** claim they have found a 5,000-year-old **UNDERWATER PYRAMID**.

In 2001
sonar images showed an
ANCIENT UNDERWATER CITY
near CUBA.

ANCIENT WONDERS

The
FIRST LIGHTHOUSE
was built around
2,400 years ago
in Egypt.
It used mirrors
to reflect light.

The **COLOSSUS** OF **RHODES**, a 12-metre (40-foot) bronze sculpture made in the 4th century BCE, was the model for the STATUE OF LIBERTY in New York City, USA.

One of the world's

LARGEST

RUBBISH DUMPS

was discovered in

Southern Italy.

It is more than 2,000 years old.

The dump contains more than 25 MILLION CLAY JARS that once held olive oil.

CLAY JARS

ANCIENT PERUVIANS MADE GIANT DRAWINGS IN THE NAZCA DESERT.

One drawing of a PELICAN is 305 metres (1,000 feet) long. That's longer than THREE FOOTBALL FIELDS!

There are more than 900 of these drawings.
They are now called the Nazca Lines.

WHO KNOWS?

About 4,000 years ago, people placed almost **3,000 LARGE STONES** in a field in France.

NO ONE KNOWS WHY.

They are now called the **CARNAC STONES.**

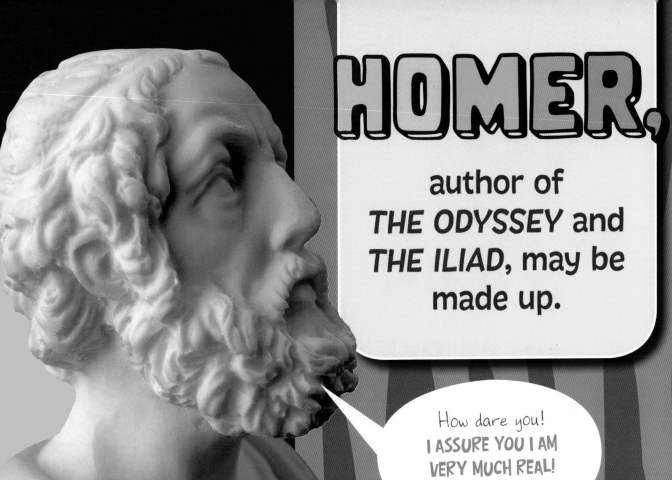

It took about **2,300,000 STONE BLOCKS** to build the **GREAT PYRAMID OF KHUFU** at **GIZA, EGYPT.**

THE THREE PYRAMIDS AT GIZA ALIGN WITH THE THREE STARS IN ORION'S BELT.

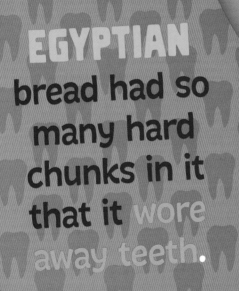

EGYPTIAN bread had so many hard chunks in it that it wore away teeth.

The **CHINESE** invented ice cream thousands of years ago.

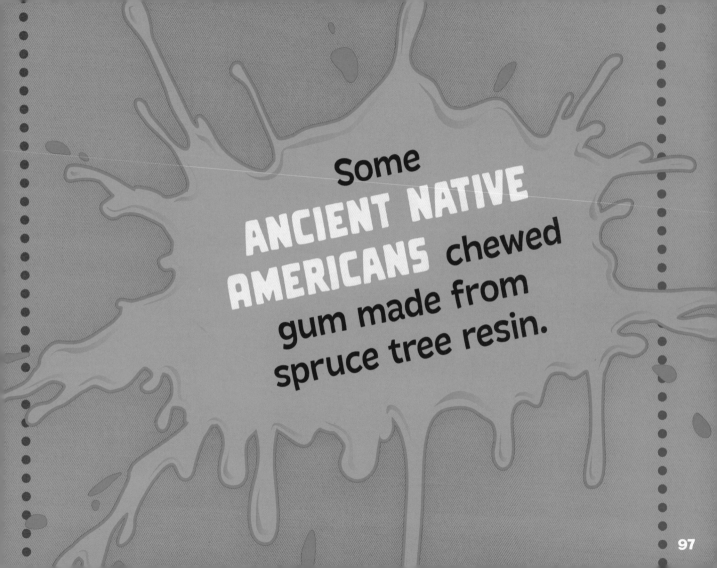

Some **ANCIENT NATIVE AMERICANS** chewed gum made from spruce tree resin.

HUMANS BEGAN MAKING INSTRUMENTS MORE THAN 40,000 YEARS AGO.

The earliest flutes were made from MAMMOTH IVORY and BIRD BONES.

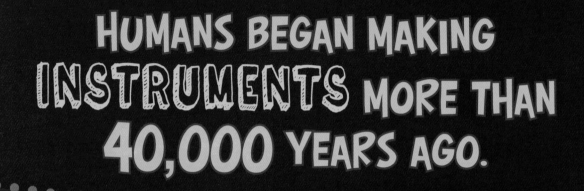

The earliest drums were made from elephant hides.

ANCIENT INCAS drilled HOLES in PEOPLE'S HEADS to relieve pain.

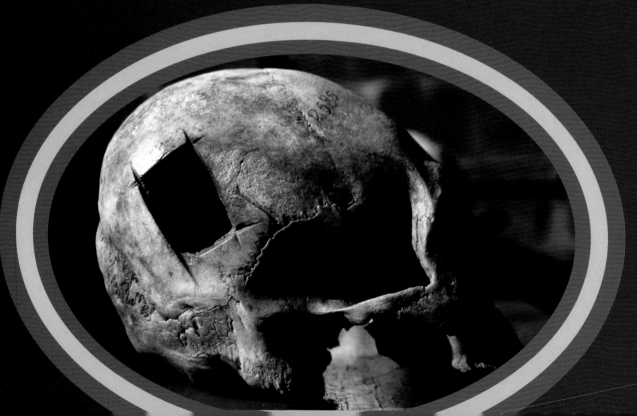

ANCIENT EGYPTIANS
placed electric eels over
painful body areas to
REDUCE THE PAIN.

To restore someone's **SIGHT**, Egyptians poured mashed red ochre, honey and pig's eye into the person's **EAR**.

Ancient Babylonian treatment for **TEETH GRINDING:** sleep next to a **SKULL**.

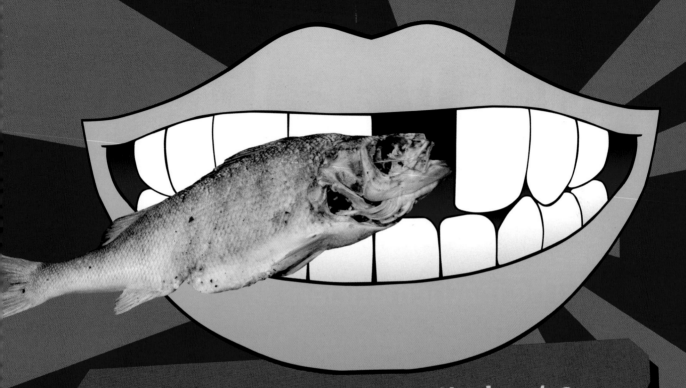

If a Roman dentist pulled out a **ROTTEN TOOTH**, he would fill the hole with **ROTTEN FISH**.

WEIRD BELIEFS!

The mathematician **PYTHAGORAS** believed that all beans were evil.

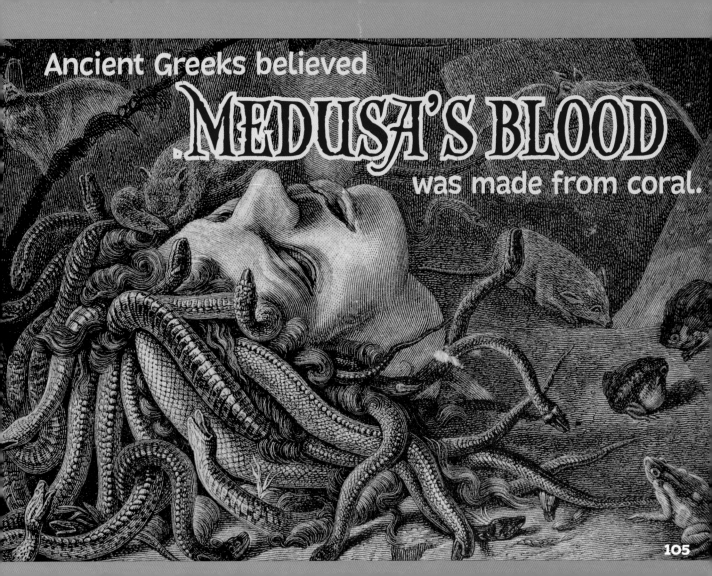

Ancient Greeks believed **MEDUSA'S BLOOD** was made from coral.

The great military leader **HANNIBAL** had 37 elephants in his army.

OTHER ANIMALS USED IN ANCIENT BATTLES:

HORSES

LIONS

ELEPHANTS

PIGS

TIGERS

MONKEYS

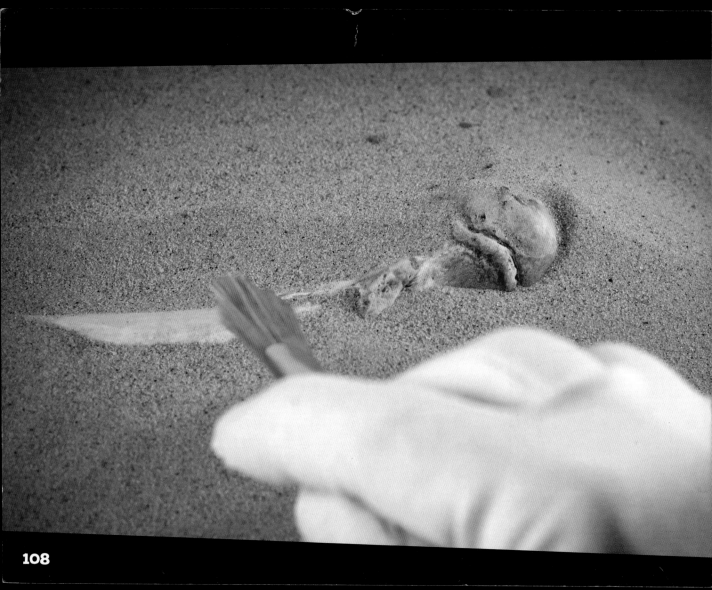

SOME **HISTORIANS** BELIEVE THAT HUMANS ALMOST WENT EXTINCT AROUND 70,000 YEARS AGO.

GLOSSARY

boomerang flat, curved wooden tool used for hunting; if it is thrown in a certain way, it will return to the thrower

cicada large insect; males make a loud shrill sound

dung animal poo

gladiator warrior who fought to the death in a Roman public arena

jade stone (usually green) that is often used for jewellery

mollusc animal, like a clam, that has a soft body; it usually lives in a shell

sacrifice act of offering something, usually a slain animal, to a god

seismograph machine that senses and measures movements in the Earth's crust

sewage waste, both liquid and solid, that is disposed of through the use of sewers or drains

suture stitch a wound together

resin sticky stuff that comes out of trees

terracotta reddish clay often put into a hot oven to make it hard

toga long, loose piece of clothing worn in ancient Rome

READ MORE

Ancient Egypt (Eyewitness), DK (DK Children, 2014)

Ancient Rome (Eyewitness), DK (DK Children, 2015)

A Visitor's Guide to Ancient Greece (Usborne Visitor Guides), Lesley Sims (Usborne Publishing, 2014)

Daily Life in Shang Dynasty China (Daily Life in Ancient Civilizations), Lori Hile (Heinemann Educational Books, 2015)

WEBSITES

www.ancientegypt.co.uk/menu.html
Learn about Egyptian life, mummies and gods and goddesses at this British Museum website.

www.bbc.co.uk/history/ancient/romans/
Read about Roman emperors and more at this BBC website.

www.childrensuniversity.manchester.ac.uk/interactives/history/greece/exploreancientgreece/
Use an interactive map to explore Ancient Greece!

INDEX

Raintree is an imprint of Capstone Global Library Limited,
a company incorporated in England and Wales having its registered office at
264 Banbury Road, Oxford, OX2 7DY – Registered company number: 6695582

www.raintree.co.uk
myorders@raintree.co.uk

Editor: Megan Atwood | Designer: Veronica Scott | Media Researcher: Jo Miller | Production Specialist: Gene Bentdahl

ISBN 978 1 4747 1286 6 (hardback)   ISBN 978 1 4747 1295 8 (paperback)
20 19 18 17 16   21 20 19 18 17
10 9 8 7 6 5 4 3 2 1   10 9 8 7 6 5 4 3 2 1

British Library Cataloguing in Publication Data
A full catalogue record for this book is available from the British Library.

Acknowledgements
We would like to thank the following for permission to reproduce photographs:
Alamy: Claudia Wiens, 72, Glyn Thomas, 89, North Wind Picture Archives, 62-63; Corbis: AS400 DB, 86, John A. Bryan, 38; Getty Images: DeAgostini/G.DAGLI ORTI/DEA, 32, SSPL, 56, UIG/Prisma, 33; Glow Images: Prisma RM/Raga Jose Fuste, 83; Newscom: akg-images, 106, akg-images/Peter Connolly, 77, akg-images/Werner Forman, 98, BAO imageBROKER, 105, Danita Delimont Photography/Adam Jones, 23, (pharaoh), EPA/Mike Nelson, 31 (mummy); Prisma/Album, 58, 71, Stock Connection USA/picturescolourlibrary.com, 13 (queen), Stock Connection USA/View Stock, 52-53, Universal Images Group Universal Images Group/Leemage, 55, (right), World History Archive, 50, 82; Science Source: Daniele Pellegrini, 100; Shutterstock: 101images, 36, A-R-T, 11, Afterfocus Studio, 69, aletermi, 103 (fish), Alex Malikov, back cover, Alex Mit, 28, (brain), Alvaro Trabazo Rivas, 7, Anastasia Koro, 23, (lava), andamanec, 66, angelinast, 95, Artem Loskutnikov, cover, (bottom left), AS Food studio, 42, Atelier Sommerland, 84-85, Baimieng, 28, (skull), Baloncici, 3, BigGabig, 8-9, Bildagentur Zoonar GmbH, 19, (hawk), Binh Thanh Bui, 31 (red onion), Binh Thanh Bui, 46, (salad), cobalt88, 94, DAIVI, 20-21, dedMazay, 75, (both), Dimitrios, 67, (right), Dja65, 29, (pot), DM7, 46, (gladiator), , cover, (top right), dogboxstudio, 44, Donavan van Staden, 99, DutchScenery, 13, (fake beard), ehtesham, 48, EKS, 54-55, Eric Isselee, 4, (camel), 18, 19, (lion and baboon), 64, 78, 79, (sheep), Everett Historical, 104, (inset), Fejas, 57, funkypoodle, 21 (rabbit cookie), garanga, 87, Gilmanshin, 67, (left), heromen30, 22, Hong Vo, 31 (orange onion), James Steidl, 25, Jeff Cameron Collingwood, 41, Joseph Calev, 60-61, Kamira, 2, 5, Ken Cook, 103 (mouth), kontur-vid, 24, (all), Kumpoi Chuansakul, 40, kzww, 81, lanych, 39, leungchopan, 27, Lukiyanova Natalia / frenta, 30, (scroll), lynea, 6, marina_ua, 12, Mariusz Szczygiel, 47, Matyas Rehak, 91, MaxShutter, 42-43, Melinda Fawver, 45, (mouse), Mikhail Zahranichny, 29, (mummy), mrjo, 34, Natalyon, 26, NRT, 28, (nose), Olga_Phoenix, 20 (pig bun), pandapaw, 79, (zebra), parmoht hongtong, 35, Piotr Wawrzyniuk, 16-17, Pixeljoy, cover, (bottom right), polat, 74, Reddogs, 45, Top, Regissercom, 30, (pharaoh), Robynrg, 4, (mule), S.Cooper Digital, 19, (ibis), Sarawut Padungkwan, 15, SeDmi, 70, Skalapendra, 68, sommai damrongpanich, 17, (necklace), Stuart Monk, 76, tanja-vashchuk, 10, 11, TristanBM, 79, (horse), udra11, 108, Vasileios Karafillidis, 93, Vasileios Karafillidis, cover, (top left), Veroncia Louro, 48-49, Virinaflora, 90, Vitaly Korovin, 79, (donkey), Voropaev Vasiliy, 49, wallnarez, 28, (eye); SuperStock: DeAgostini, 14, Wikimedia: cat diary, 28, (jade cicada)

Design Elements by Capstone and Shutterstock

Printed and bound in China.